MOVING THE BONES

Poems

RICK BAROT

MILKWEED EDITIONS

Published 2024 by Milkweed Editions
Printed in Canada
Cover design by Mary Austin Speaker
Cover art by Sophie Taeuber-Arp
Author photo by Jason Comerford
24 25 26 27 28   5 4 3 2 1
First Edition

Library of Congress Cataloging-in-Publication Data

Names: Barot, Rick, 1969- author.
Title: Moving the bones : poems / by Rick Barot.
Description: First edition. | Minneapolis, Minnesota : Milkweed Editions, 2024. | Summary: "A vulnerable and honest collection of poems exploring lineage, love, and the pandemic, from one of the most acclaimed poets of his generation"-- Provided by publisher.
Identifiers: LCCN 2023059519 (print) | LCCN 2023059520 (ebook) | ISBN 9781571315649 (paperback) | ISBN 9781571317889 (ebook)
Subjects: LCGFT: Poetry.
Classification: LCC PS3602.A835 M68 2024 (print) | LCC PS3602.A835 (ebook) | DDC 811/.6--dc23/eng/20231228
LC record available at https://lccn.loc.gov/2023059519
LC ebook record available at https://lccn.loc.gov/2023059520

Milkweed Editions is committed to ecological stewardship. We strive to align our book production practices with this principle, and to reduce the impact of our operations in the environment. We are a member of the Green Press Initiative, a nonprofit coalition of publishers, manufacturers, and authors working to protect the world's endangered forests and conserve natural resources. *Moving the Bones* was printed on acid-free 100% postconsumer-waste paper by Friesens Corporation.

Edgar Alvarez Barot, 1943–2023
for my father, in memoriam

CONTENTS

Each statue will be broken
if the heart is a temple.

~AGHA SHAHID ALI

MOVING THE BONES

PLEASURE

You are told to believe in one paradise
and then there is the paradise you come to know.
The shoes lined up in pairs by the door
and the herd moving with its mysterious intent
across a dark plain. The blue of the sky
which is the zenith of all colors
and the love of the man in the next room,
strong and rough as a hog's back.
My mind has a slow metabolism, it is slow
to understand what anything means,
but it understands that if you look at something
long enough, it will have something
to say to you. The sun that is strangely bright
on some days, a poisoned canary,
and the crop of winter rocks in a meadow
in April. Learning decades later
the name of the hospital where you were born
and watching the child eat a mango
as though it is time he is eating, time shining
on his lips. On fewer days I agree
with the poet's dread of being
the wrong person in the right world, and believe
in adhesion, in never showing up
empty-handed, even if the pleasure I know best
is fused with the abject. There is always
the other side of the heart, its coaxing:
You are here. You can begin again. You can rise.

THE LOVERS

One of them is still there in the smell of burnt toast
        and dirty clothes that was my twenties, always waiting
to be picked up outside some station, that tenderness
set against each building's law of metal and stone.

One of them is still on a slope of the Sandias,
jeans pushed down to his knees
        so I can pick out the cactus needles from his thigh.
        The sky is late, the color of grape soda. In weeks he will go
to a war, write letters that now sleep in a box
in the basement, next to a box of Christmas ornaments.

I open a book I read in college
        and one of them is in the margins, his handwriting
an enthusiastic vine, like the vines at the edges
of medieval texts, each *o* of his cursive a tiny horse chestnut,
        the paperback's pages yellow as a smoker's fingers.

Another one is still on his motorcycle
between Connecticut and Manhattan, driving a cab on weekends
for his tuition. On the nights I rode behind him,
        my head against the black leather of his back, I knew
I would die many times before my death.

One death for the one walking down Iowa Avenue,
        brooding on the problem of wearing a jacket
over a Halloween costume. One death
for the one scorned by his parents and brothers.

One death for the one locked for days in his room, drawing lines
in a notebook, over and over and over.

Standing in front of a glass case in a museum, he is beside me,
looking at the silver hand
resting like a claw on the gray velvet.
Another one is in his grandfather's miles of orchards,
a place more immense because he is a boy
lost in it, even though everything he sees is his kingdom.

There is no logic in what we keep.
The freckles on his forearms. The surgery scar
on his shoulder. The reliquary that outlasts the bone of the saint.

In the coffeehouse I see them, the lovers,
the two teenage boys on a couch,
cuddling into one fused shape, one boy holding a phone
they lean toward, their faces lit by the platinum glow.
I have been them, and whatever comes after,

and it has taken all my heart to contain both.
There is no logic in what we keep, even of ourselves.

I am near him on a winter beach, the sky above shining like coal.
I am sitting with him on a sidewalk
and he is weeping. I am alone in a hotel room,
thinking of all the ice machines on every floor of every hotel
in the world, the sad machines dreaming
of each pure cube of light.

GOODWILL

When I put the small cobalt vase into the shopping basket,
he tells me I had donated that same vase

to that same Goodwill months ago, mocking me only a little
for not remembering. Last night I watched him

put halved plums on a baking dish, shake brown sugar
and fresh thyme over them, add a bit

of water, and roast them until they sank into soft sweetness.
A few weeks ago I talked to my mother

about the different kinds of portable urinals she might buy
to use during her recovery, our grief and mirth

at the one that looked like a garbage bag
you slipped onto yourself. There was the long moment, too,

when I stood before the linden tree by the parking lot
on campus, asking it what it had seen

during the year everyone disappeared, like a tree thriving
inside a ruined, roofless cathedral. This summer

we sat outside and talked about those
who had died. He had been a bank manager and stole money

and left the country. She had had an affair with a priest.
The afternoon, like gossip turning into legend,

got dark. In the winter, in my dreams,
people would appear, their complexions dry and gray

as mushrooms. They asked for directions
or stood at the wall while I did some task that would never

be finished. I didn't know these people
but understood they knew me, like ghosts, like ancestors,

their old desires thick in our new desires.
It isn't that I had forgotten giving it away. It's that I wanted

the blue vase back, having lost it that once.
This morning I watched him lie in bed without clothes

and knew the pungence of every fold
of his body, the way your fingers smell after rubbing

some thyme. A sprinkler was on outside,
a sound like a jump rope on the sidewalk. Then the sound

of children, the neighbor's children, leading me
to that ladder within the self, with the boy

on a low rung, the man on the middle rungs, and the old man
above us, touching the leaves of the tree.

THE BOY WITH A FLOWER BEHIND HIS EAR

1.

When you have been on trains on buses on the road with someone
for months living with each other's filthy teenager things you don't

expect him to come up with a neat shirt and black trousers from
the bottom of his backpack on the last night which is what he did

looking like a waiter his hair windblown across continents now cut
as if for a ceremony his blue eyes like the summer's oceans but

before the dinner and the next morning's flights to separate places
we have to go find Karl Marx's grave taking the underground across

the city walking under the rippling trees of the cemetery the green
of the place like cinematography and finally we are standing in front

of the famous man's enormous bronze head and I am looking at him
looking at it I am looking at the side of his smiling face his ear

and the speck of shaving cream I point out to him wanting to touch
him there thirty years his white shirt ahead of me on the path back.

2.

On the podcast the psychologist talking about death and our need
to accept death describes a state he calls an anticipatory resoluteness

with solicitous regard for others that will make your life seem an
adventure profused with unshakable joy those were his exact words

I wrote them down understanding that what needed such breathless
saying I have brought to one word *you* the one word encompassing

all language all tasks all meaning *you* like those saints in paintings
working with a skull on their desks like the psychologist saying that

the knowledge of death makes for an enlightened life but instead
of knowledge or a skull on my desk there is *you* and the little blur

the little flicker the little bloom of it on the page *you* which is only to
say he was right the scholar of poetry who insisted that the work

of poetry is the work of preserving the fact of the beloved the *you* of
the beloved the work of poetry is preserving the face of the beloved.

3.

Like the boy with a flower behind his ear who's been interrupted
in his pleasure a pleasure first figured in the sprigs of jasmine and

rose in a round clear vase on the table the water in the vase so full
as though it's just been filled the leaves of the flowers also full

of the glossiness of the clean water and of the plums and cherries
also on the table the fruit rendered by the painter in a tumbling

cascade just at the base of the boy's torso where the painting is
in shadow is shadowed with a kind of privacy the last and long

part of your looking where you will finally notice the boy's finger
bitten by the lizard still dangling from the finger the lizard that

must have emerged like a snake from the Eden of those fruits
the boy's recoil figured in the gasp of the mouth and the shoulder

torqued from its white blouse the shoulder that's also jasmine and
rose in the Roman sunlight describing it these four hundred years.

THE STREETS

When he came back from the streets he said
that everyone had worn masks, the stores
had all been boarded up, and the cops had
their gear and their shields, so that everything
was muffled while also terrible, terrifying.
He saw a woman, an older white woman,
get shoved down and she stayed down, curled
up, until she was helped. Because I was sick
and couldn't go there, I had the luxury
of seeing the woman as an image, a seashell
or an ampersand on the ground, though I didn't
tell him this. He saw the tents people lived in
by the park get torched, and I could smell
on him what he had seen. There were people
with bullhorns you couldn't really hear.
There was singing along with the chanting
of all the names of those who were murdered.
He said it didn't matter what kind of day
it was but it was ironic that it was a beautiful
summer day, the sky a swimming pool.
He lost the two friends he had gone with.
Though they'd told each other to meet in front
of the public library if they got separated,
the crowd had gotten thick and angry there.
At the crowd's edges were people selling
t-shirts, books, and water, like the commerce
that sprang up at the edges of battlefields.
But it wasn't a war, he said, because he

could walk away from it and take the bus
back home. I thought of him looking like a boy
looking out the window, the tilt of late sun
a hand smoothing a tablecloth. I thought
of the bus the way I thought of poems, that it
was a civic space and a lyric space at once.
I knew not to say any more about what
I was only imagining. He turned and went
to the other room, to wash his hands and face.

TO J.

These stories are told as penance, lifted by tongues and said
into the sea so that we may be new again.
At the bottom of the cliff, our pants are dusty and our palms
stained from the orange dirt bright as children's
cereal. We have chosen to trade what is familiar behind us
for what is before us—the fog's thickness muting
shadows in its abrupt approach, objects made plain
as salt laced on the rocks. I squat above a tidal pool and stare
into the circle. Because we must gather images
to construct truths, the sea is beautiful and then it is
frightening. At first: *It's only an anemone.* Then: *Prepare for rage.*
The tide aches. The largeness of the day distorts
our sense of scale, what we can know. I will remember
this place to be no larger than a shoebox packed with stones.
Your voice. It cannot travel now across that water.

CROSSHATCH 1

I stood before it. The rectangle of gray wax on the canvas, its expanse
a kind of pastoral. The teeth marks in its center, the painting an apple.

    I stood there, as though inside an idea materializing. Johns said, "Take
    an object. Do something to it. Do something else to it." Paint it, then eat it.

A painting like the back of the man wearing a black coat. A painting
like a piece of paper repeatedly stepped-on on a sidewalk. A painting

    like the purple foil balloon caught in the yellow ginkgo tree. A painting
    like a chorale. A painting like people moving with flashlights in a forest.

The ekphrastic act is a catalyst for observation, association, and dream.
It is like the flaneur's arc of walking, seeing, and reverie. I see you

    move down the busy block before you have seen me and I look away,
    to make another image in my mind, to have it take the force of the blow.

If I were like that ivory hippopotamus on whom the Egyptian artist
has etched the reeds where the actual hippopotamus would have stood,

    hidden in its element, I would have on my body the names of every
    beloved, each sweet chemical burn, like a drop of vanilla on the tongue.

The piazza was imperceptibly concave, like an enormous shallow bowl.
People sat there in clusters, as though having a picnic on grass instead

    of cobblestones. Centuries of earthquakes had struck the church, but on
    one wall whose fresco was otherwise gone: a thigh pierced by an arrow.

One of them takes his bedsheet and paints a flag on it. The other takes
his pillow and quilt and fixes them to canvas. Sleep, dream, and work

equal love. The grimy window like a calendar, paint on the floors like
notes on staves. As Constable said: painting is another word for feeling.

Like looking into someone's desk drawer when they are away or after
they have died: stencils, newspapers, beeswax, enamel, tin cups, spoons,

broom, ruler, flags, busted chair, mannequin leg. Each defining what
Johns said of the poetic: "something that conveys many meanings at once."

To know something you have to describe it, or praise it, or fear it, or turn
aside from it, in a precise gathering of contradictions. In the painting

of the three magi, one king kneeling in front of Mary and the baby Christ
has first taken off his crown, which is now on the ground beside him.

The ocean is so large it doesn't have to know what it is. Yet it desires
to know its own boundaries the way a tree does, or a mouse, or a house.

I am a mud man. I am made of mud. I think of mud the way a lightbulb
is preoccupied with light, the way the water is preoccupied with the shore.

Crosshatch of scent. Crosshatch of light snow. Crosshatch of cicadas.
Crosshatch of the mirror and crosshatch of the corpse. Crosshatch

of the tantric detail. Crosshatch of dancers on a plane. Crosshatch
of weeping women. Crosshatch of the clock and crosshatch of the bed.

MY REMBRANDT

Because I have reached the age that he is
in the painting, I cannot mock him. I understand the wish
for a kind of glamour

in the jeweled tunic he is wearing, golden as a lion.
The fur cape looks just about
to fall off his shoulders, as though he bore the weight

of his own importance with easy disregard.
And that silver-capped walking stick, like a scepter.
Only his amused and sad eyes

hold the trouble that has become his life—
the bankruptcy, the grand house
sold off that same year, the wonder-cabinet amazements

auctioned, and the move to the small
house in the unfashionable district, its rooms damp
as potato peels. Behind the story told

by the painting, another story, like the ostentatious black
background surrounding him. I look past
his shoulder and what's there is a sensation

that is not oblivion but fortune,
and filled with my own images. When I was a child,
we stood on the shore in the dark and watched

the fishermen walk into the calm low tide
of the bay, a lantern in one hand, small spear in the other,
bent down, as though they had lost something.

Before I was led into the operating room,
the nurse gave me a Sharpie to write
a *yes* on my belly, where the surgeons did their work.

I dream of greenhouses of flowering geraniums.
Not an hour goes by when I don't see my parents' faces
in my eyes, a lighthouse beam

cutting regularly through the clutter.
In the painting he is fifty-two, his fame still flashing
through the city like the red sash across his tunic.

The painting is the largest self-portrait
he will paint, a way of outwitting shame, because shame
is a small thing, a thing you can outwit,

or transform into something else. He died in 1669,
I was born in 1969. I have lost
only what I intended to lose, or was not brave enough

to fight for. I have no wife, no son,
but a remembering that is its own wonder cabinet.
Once, at a window in Venice, I saw a barge with a coffin

go past on the canal. Once, sick for home,
I read the page in the novel that described all the terms
for rice in my first language:

sapaw, tukol, kumag, tahip, palay, bugas,
ipa, kan-on, am, goto, suam, bahog, apa, busa, ampaw, malagkit,
kata, saing, bahaw, tukag. Once,

I stood at the curb outside my house
and saw the coyote on the street, its pauper's grandeur,
a form in the wash of the streetlight, then gone.

DURING THE PANDEMIC

1.

During the pandemic, I thought of abstract art. Abstract art, the art historian claimed, was the most democratic kind of art because it allowed for anyone's interpretations, anyone's feelings. You didn't have to know anything to get it. For instance, the canvas that was painted uniformly black could be open-ended and be a consensus at the same time. Like a plague.

2.

During the pandemic, I watched the weather. The sky brought forth its clean clouds. The trees put forth their green like store awnings. You could go online and look at places in every weather. I loved best the weather that was ours. Rain that fell so hard it sounded like a crowd. Ours, like a postcard in the mail or the sparklers on a cake. It was spring, a rash season. Then the sun on everything. "The sun never knew how great it was," the architect said, "until it hit the side of a building."

3.

During the pandemic, I fixed on each fear. Each fear was its own
fastidiousness. My mother and her fear of the ocean, not even
a touch of it, not even her feet in the tender edge of surf. My
friend and his fear of tunnels, the tunnels he went through with
his eyes closed. When we went outside we wore latex gloves the
colors of Easter. We stood apart in the mandated distance, like the
remaining pieces at the end of a game of chess.

4.

During the pandemic, I followed each impulse as it turned into a procedure. I bought a can of peaches because I read a novel in which it figured as a metaphor. I separated the stuff inside a drawer, like a TV dinner and its neat portions. I looked at photographs and suddenly understood that a photograph was a letter to someone in the future. In one photograph, he stands in front of the cinder block pattern of a wall, his hair still brown, his red sweatshirt draped over his shoulder like a bloody pelt.

5.

During the pandemic, I noticed the pencils. One kept a window open a crack. Another held up the tendril growing out of the avocado seed in a cup. One waited on my nightstand next to a pad of hotel stationery. The hotel had been by the interstate cutting across the middle of the map. Driving from one end of the country to the other, I knew I was in the thick of my own story. I looked down to the lit hotel pool. Even though it was late, there were people there, caught in gestures that made me think of Pompeii.

6.

During the pandemic, I knew we were in a period of interval so I considered what an interval meant. The interval we were in was not like swinging in a hammock on a warm afternoon. It was not like making a lesson plan to be taught. It was not even like being inside a car wash and its cleansing tempest. It was more like Lucky's speech in the middle of Beckett's play, its torrent of rage and grief, after which the waiting, which was the point after all, resumed.

7.

During the pandemic, I lost the little lusts that were the sugar cubes of each day. Pornographic lusts. Vending machine lusts. Ambition lusts. They were now like flowers pressed to transparence in a book of philosophy. I devoured sleep and sentences. "Life is a game and true love is a trophy," the singer sang, all silvery. Who knew what was true now? Death tolls. Or those dolphins returning to the empty canals of Venice.

8.

During the pandemic, I learned the half hour of sun that slanted into one side of my room, the light like a giant wing. I would lie on the floor and read heavy books, surprised by the legs of furniture. The stumpy legs of a stool, the giraffe legs of a table. On days when there was no sun, I sat there and looked up at the window, at the sky that was the color of a sidewalk.

9.

During the pandemic, I read a book about glaciation in the Pacific Northwest. I read a book about a composer's life, the agony that was each of his symphonies. I read a book about moss. Everything was basically about time. I meticulously dusted the leaves of my houseplant with a tissue. This gesture was one kind of time. I imagined where I stood as it would have been 15,000 years ago, the glacier a mile high in thickness. This was another kind of time. I imagined the ice, traveling through its geology in a luminous round enclosure, as though the past were science fiction.

10.

During the pandemic, I knew each neighbor by one thing. The neighbors above, the baby. The neighbors below, the dog. Someone down the hall, fried fish. Someone else down the hall, the opera when their door opened. I made my rooms quieter by standing in the middle of each one, my mind moving intently, like an old man in slippers. I wondered what one thing the neighbors would know me by. What truth an inadvertence could betray.

11.

During the pandemic, I had dreams. I gave a lecture inside a stadium with only my voice. I was small and lived within a keyhole. I walked on a pilgrimage trail with my pack gaining a new item each day. I would wake with sour eyes. My sister called to ask what had become of my money. My friend called to ask if I needed groceries. Each conversation was like dreaming in a dream, like being inside an egg's slushy light.

12.

During the pandemic, I understood how far away I was from things I once knew with forensic intensity. How the French parliamentary system worked. The tempers of one man's face. Differential equations. I had time to think of the turn at the heart of each thing. *Abandon*, for example. That it could mean *free and unfettered* in one usage. And, in another, *leave behind*.

13.

During the pandemic, I listened. Things hummed their tunes. The pear. The black sneaker. The old-fashioned thermometer. The stapler with the face of a general from eastern Europe. Once, my father confessed he had taken the padlock from his factory locker and clipped it on the rail of a footbridge at the park. He had retired. The park was near his house. Each time he went there, I imagined him feeling pleased, going to work.

14.

During the pandemic, I kept a list of possible symptoms on the refrigerator door. From a distance it looked like a shopping list, an ersatz normalcy. Fever instead of flour, cough instead of bacon, fatigue instead of milk. With each day, the slippages proliferated. Hospital instead of hospitality, projections instead of protections, virus instead of virtue. Asymptomatic veered toward asymptote, an intimate infinity between them.

15.

During the pandemic, I sat with hunger, I sat with nostalgia. Hunger was predictable, its glucose durations. Nostalgia took one form as the horse-drawn tartanilla that brought us from the dock to our house. It was dawn. We had been on a boat all night, a crossing. Now we were on another conveyance as sleepy as another century. This was in another country.

16.

During the pandemic, I looked out the window at the moment
a runner went by. His stride had an exaggerated beauty, like
everything that was outside of my mind. The blue recycling
dumpster. The white cereal bowl. The pink full moon. Inside
my mind was woe, an attic full of gray insulation. "Another
day, another dolor," said the poet, sad and drunk, looking at
the pigeons outside his window at the Chelsea Hotel.

17.

During the pandemic, I thought of what people thought they needed. Bread and bleach and guns. The toilet paper aisle laid bare as a cathedral. In his hurried texts, my friend kept saying *lost* when he meant *lots*. He was sick already, did not want to be sick twice over. We dreaded all the minute, unseen mechanisms. Malign surfaces. Malign particles. Malign cells. We washed the apples with soap and water.

18.

During the pandemic, I came to understand that excess is the first quality of the imagination. Like newspapers writing the obituaries of the famous ahead of their actual deaths. Like the child who takes his crayon and draws a door on the wall, thinking he can turn the knob and go somewhere else.

19.

During the pandemic, I wanted to take up as little space as possible. Wake, wash, eat, clean, watch, lie: I wanted my habits reduced to a ritual of monosyllables. "A skull is a beautiful structure, and used to waiting," the painter said. I admired the painter's suave severity. That grim style. Now that isolation and obedience were what I knew of refuge.

20.

During the pandemic, I watched the screen of my phone as he moved his phone around the outboard engine he had brought inside, cleaning it, tinkering with it. The thing looked like sculpture: shiny in parts, in parts streaked with grease. He was states away. When his face returned to the screen, it was smudged from what he had been doing. Don't touch your face, I lamely said, touching the screen, cut by the terms of our separation: adoration and sorrow, sweet and bitter.

21.

During the pandemic, I prayed as I had not since childhood. I prayed for him, for her, for her, for her, for her, for him. We didn't know what the day would bring, like the uncle holding out two closed fists, a bullet in one of them. Like God, each day unfolded and spread without definition. God of the moonlight flooding the empty parking lot. God of the paintings in the dim museums, missing the voices of schoolchildren.

22.

During the pandemic, I thought of scale. Pandemics, I read, had shaped human history from the start, like lava scorching an old landscape with regularity. This was one kind of scale. The tweet from the man announcing his wife's death from the virus was another kind of scale. Soft, the size of my face, the mask I wore to the store was one kind of scale. The racist violence being done to people who looked like me was another. "The poem is the speech of citizenship," a scholar wrote. And I laughed.

23.

During the pandemic, I couldn't distinguish between solitude and loneliness, between trivia and news, between restraint and prohibition. I went to the barren track of the high school and felt as a mending, walking around in circles. The gulls above looked like scissors. I thought of how we thought of nature as an infinity. This was part of the calamity.

24.

During the pandemic, I reflected on how time had different properties for different things. Time and the dragonfly. Time and the diamond. Time and the rough button of skin at my lover's elbow. Time and the smiling stick figure in the painting by Klee. "The virtues of a thing do not come from it: they go to it," wrote the clerk, writing poems in the print shop during the day, saying the poems to himself as he walked home in the evenings of Buenos Aires.

25.

During the pandemic, I wondered about the double lives of punctuation. The semicolon as the subway turnstile. The book ends of the parentheses. The streetlight at the end of the dark street that was the period. The dash of millinery that was *l'accent aigu*. I made a pot of white beans and a pig's foot, a monstrous comma in a winter of words.

26.

During the pandemic, I mapped out itineraries so I could make my way through them. Walking the thirteen miles of Broadway from Inwood to Bowling Green. Riding the BART train from Richmond to Fremont. Starting out in Hampstead then walking the miles into London with Keats. I considered what I would need. Snacks, money. A light-tan jacket, like my grandfather wore in spring. The blue and green plaid of its lining.

27.

During the pandemic, I went outside as into an abstraction, every body a vector, every public space a possible inflection point, the very air a moral injury. But there was no abstracting this: the bus driver died. The shoemaker. The chef. The playwright. The nurses and the doctors. The ambassador. The princess. The leader of the band. The scholar of Derrida.

28.

During the pandemic, I was alone. I had chosen to be. I could have gone there or there or there and sheltered with those I loved, but what I loved and what I chose did not always correlate in my character. This was a point of pride or a fault, depending. "The Greek word *character* means trademark—a potter's mark on the underside of a vase," noted the classicist.

29.

During the pandemic, I praised the cherry blossoms. I praised my lungs. I praised crying. I praised the faces of my students checkerboarded on the computer screen. I praised the curses I gave to those who deserved them. I praised coffee. I praised ventilators. I praised the people gathered on the rooftop of a nearby building, laughing as they looked at the night sky.

30.

During the pandemic, I had days when I felt I was by myself on a shore drained of the tide, dragging a stick across miles of wet sand. There were also days when I was a boy again, sliding down a snowy hill on a flattened cardboard box. And there were days when I remembered the teacher who made us memorize a poem each week, and when we asked why, she said we might one day find ourselves in a wreck at the side of the road and we would recite these poems to stay alive.

MOVING THE BONES

There are too many ancestors, so we are gathering their bones.

The poor ones, their graves broken by the roots of trees. The ones whose headstones have been weathered as blank as snowdrifts.

We have bought the wide plot. We have built the mausoleum. And now we fill it with the bones.

The ones killed in the monsoon floods. The one buried in her wedding dress. The one buried with his medals.

Because there will be a time when we cannot keep track of them, scattered in the cemetery like prodigals, we collect the bones.

The ones whose faces I can still recall. The ones who have been dead for a hundred years. We collect their bones.

At each opened grave, we think about the body taking its shape as *father, sister, cousin, uncle.* We hunger for the story of each figure.

We hold the bones, though we know memory is mostly forgetting. Or memory is the sweeper who clears the sidewalk each morning. Or memory is the broom.

The mausoleum is marble, white as certain roses, and shaped like a house. There is room for everyone we will put there.

The rich ones, their gravestones glowing with gold paint. The infants with sweet names. We open their graves. We move their bones.

Look back far enough and your family becomes unfamiliar, a circle of people with a fading circumference.

When I think of it long enough, *home* becomes a confusion of *birthplace, hometown, country,* and *nation.*

We walk through the cemetery, we point to our own, and we gather their bones.

Maybe memory is the desperate pharaoh who commands that the things of this life go with him into the next.

I would take with me the books I loved best. A jar of the ocean spanning my two countries. A slip of my lover's sunny hair.

I would take with me a sack of rice. My mother's orange shawl. The robe my father wears in the kitchen at night, drinking a glass of water.

That we might go to just one place to worship them, to wonder at who they were, we are moving the bones.

Our tribe of eros and vinegar. Our black hair, our ordinary minds.

Holding the bones, we say the names of the dead, the music of the syllables, conjuring the hearts they answered to. We hold the bones.

Each stern skull. Each proud sternum. Each elegant rib, curved like a horizon.

ABUNDANCE

It must say something wonderful about my life
that my first meal in America was a bucket

of chicken from Kentucky Fried Chicken.
I was ten. Hours before, the arrival at the airport

to the cacophony of relatives, then the drive
to my uncle's house in the new winter cold,

where the bucket waited, like America itself.
For once, that one memory is not like the tattered

band t-shirt you only wear to bed, but like
the crisp task the teacher gives to her students.

She hands each of us a mason jar full of black,
white, red, and brown rice. She tells us

to pour the rice on the table and sort it
by color, however long it will take. In this way

the counting and accounting, like the work
of memory, is its own abundance, along with that

of the gorgeous rice. All my life I have been
drawn to exercises in patience because so many

of the things I love don't love me back, a claim
that, to borrow an aching line from Miłosz,

I make not out of sorrow but in wonder.
The patience of bending over a table, counting.

The patience of hunger. The patience of love
clinging to an image of sunlight on a hazel eye.

That day, we lay on the summer time grass
of the park and looked up at the maples

the sun ruffled through. He told me about
the stern way his grandmother had taught him

how to play the violin when he was a child.
I told him about my childhood newspaper route,

walking the neighborhood's sleeping streets
at dawn, my hands black from newsprint,

stung by the rubber bands that always snapped.
When we weren't talking about those things

we were talking about poetry, beside ourselves
when reading out loud the Larkin poem

about how parents fuck you up, whisperingly
amazed reading Dickinson's poem about

how things fall apart in an exact, organized
decay. Reading the poems with someone else,

I had the thought that it was best to always
read poems this way, like the trains in Europe

where you have to sit facing each other.
I had the thought that the space between

the lines in a poem was like the space between
two people facing each other on a bed,

the space of breath. In the park, the maples
we lay under were Norway maples, a species

considered invasive because it out-shades
everything around it. I didn't know this

when I fell in love with the geometry of each
astral leaf, or fell in love with the chorus

the leaves made when the breezes conducted
them. Often I am moved by all the information

I've gathered but don't know what to do with.
That the needles used for upholstery are curved

like parentheses. That there's a star somewhere
two hundred times bigger than our sun.

That far back in its etymology the closet
actually meant a space of intimate privacy

where you might welcome others, not a place
of shame you're supposed to leave behind.

The abundance of that closet, crowded now
with my fierce friends. The abundance

of having a new truth in the mind, the bloom
in your senses like biting into a fennel seed.

The abundance of America, its orchards
and its libraries, its cemeteries and its airports,

the circle of people praying in the basement
of a church and the muddy field after a festival,

the boy counting the sixty-seven rings
of the fresh-cut log washed up on the beach

and the girl wearing red sunglasses on the train
in the morning, startled awake at her stop,

then, like all of us, walking into the day,
into the one thing there's plenty of: the future.

OF ERRANDS

On a table in the living room
there is a gray ceramic bowl that catches
the light each afternoon, contains it.
This is the room we turned into
the room of her dying, the hospital bed
in the center, the medical equipment
against the walls like personnel.
In Maine, once, I rented a house hundreds
of years old. One room had been
the birthing room, I was told, and I sat
in that room writing toward the bright
new world I am always trying
to write into. And while I could stop
there, with those two recognitions
of endings and beginnings, I'm thinking
of yesterday's afternoon of errands.
My father and mother were in the backseat,
my sister in the passenger seat,
and I driving. It was like decades ago
but everyone in the wrong places,
as though time was simply about
different arrangements of proximity.
Sometimes someone is in front of you.
Or they are beside. At other times
they are behind you, or just elsewhere,
inconsolably, as though time was
about how well or badly you attended

to the bodies around you. First, we went
to the bakery. Then the hardware store.
The pharmacy, the grocery. Then the bank.

THE SINGING

There are eight of us in the waiting room
of the service department in the car dealership.
Some are reading newspapers, or scrolling on their phones,
or watching the TV with the news on, the sound
off. There's a woman sitting in the corner
looking down at her phone. She is humming, very softly.
The room is more like a lounge just off the lobby
of a nice hotel, with tall plants and couches.
I am reading paperwork for my job, one part of my mind
thinking about that, another part thinking
about the things the mechanic might find wrong
with my car, acting like it has a bad cough.
The humming woman is sitting near enough
that I can hear her humming begin to take on words
in a language I don't know. It sounds
like an African language, its soft registers making me think
the woman is singing a lullaby or a nostalgic song
about a landscape, though for all I know
she might be singing about a war or the clanging streets
of a city. In the half hour all of us are there
together, no one entering the room, no one called away,
the woman's humming begins to turn
insistently into singing. As her voice gets louder and lifts
into what must be the song's sad ecstasy,
an equal disquiet seems to thicken the air of the room.
Everyone is listening. No one is looking
at her, but everyone is now aware that she is there,
brought into this consensus. At first the singing

is a novel kind of delight. The unabashed woman is a story
we will get to tell about later. But as it goes on,
demanding our attention, it becomes another thing.
In one part of the room is a coffee station. In another part
is a popcorn machine where you can help
yourself to little bags of popcorn. On the TV, the face
of the man speaking looks like a square of ham.
The woman is looking down at her phone
and singing. It is the same song, looping, the same eerie
rise and fall. Someone, I think, will walk to her and tell her
to stop. Someone, I think, will tell someone
in the car dealership to make her stop. Someone will call
the police, or think of doing so, as one part
of my mind is doing now, crouched in a declivity
of shame. With kind curiosity, I also want
to go to the woman and ask her what the song is about.
One span of the song sounds like a scorched house,
while another quavers upward, as when
the plane sharply banks, filling the window with the sky.
No one in the room has moved for a long time.
There is no resolving the moment until it ends.
Whether the woman is aware of the rest of us, she does not
give any indication by lowering her voice.
She sings. She sings. She sings. She sings.

THE MUSSEL

One way of being hidden
is to be in plain sight, looking like a black rock
among other rocks in a streambed.
Another way is to be small

and latch on to the fins and gills
of fish and travel up rapids,
up rivers, across lakes, then let go,
away from the home that is every beginning.

Still another way is to live
so long you outlive counting,
like the pine twisted into its thousand
years, like the cousin species deep in the silt

of its two centuries. Another way
of being hidden is to be a part
of something large, a speck in the vibrating
web of water and earth.

And still another way is to be
quiet and rare, the gold
of broken places, though what we might see
as love continues in the fire, rain,

snow, light, and pollen that keep their touch
on those broken places.

One more way of being hidden
is to close so completely you contain

the world's dreaming, the skies
of that sleep glowing like nacre: faintly blue,
as though it were water,
faintly pink, the eyeshadow of spring.

SATELLITE

I look up from the book I am reading.
How many times in my life
have I felt the hard and painful love
I am feeling now? I don't know where he is
but I can see him: helping his uncle
clear the disorder from a part
of their land, strumming his guitar
with the handle of a worn paintbrush.
On a wall near me is a photograph
of the young monk, his back to us, looking
over a temple's balcony to the parched
valley below. His robes are red,
like a cardinal. The mountains
in the background are half in clouds,
a border between realms. In the book
I am reading, the old artist
is at her own border: seeing her grandsons
walk through the exhibit of her
work, the column of each saturated
sculpture like an abstract totem pole,
and thinking of her ancestor,
an 18-year-old who captained a cargo boat
up and down the coast, dashing
in her imagination and mine. How many
men have I lost my life to,
each bit of losing a kind of willed spite
toward my own weakness? Days ago
we stood at the dark coast

and listened to the low waves
meeting the shore. In the dark, how near
he was felt like a small force
at my shoulder, as though we were held
in the scoop of a nest. To the left
was the half-moon, casting a gold track
on the ocean. To the right, higher
above, the stars that made the Big Dipper,
the only thing we knew
to recognize, unclear on what was star,
what was planet, what was satellite.

CROSSHATCH 2

A painting like a forest of kelp under the sea. A painting like the black
heap of a collapsed piano. A painting like the traffic on the avenue,

> moving in slow, peristaltic life. A painting like blue roses, gray roses.
> A painting like white trees, the copse of hushed ideas in the mind.

There will be time to get it right. And so, over years, he works a thought
repeatedly. This shows that identity is what you can't help but express

> over and over. Identity is repetition. The self is maps. The self is numbers.
> The self is a string between eternities. There will be time to get it right.

Once, I lived in a district of a city that was like being in a series of blue
velvet rooms in a mansion. I read four books in a row that quoted

> Sontag. The books were as different as the seasons. It was winter, naked,
> like what Sontag said on page 33: "Death is the opposite of everything."

What stories lie in paintings? In Rembrandt's portrait of Jean Pellicorne
and his son, the son is four years old. It is 1632, and the painting is about

> Pellicorne's riches and his wish for riches for his son. A bag of money
> passes between their hands. The son, who would later trade in slaves.

In my mind, in the map of my neighborhood, here is the teriyaki place,
the drugstore, the church. Here is the market where the Samoan men shop

> on weekends, wearing sarongs. Here is the house with the Confederate
> flag on a pole in the front yard. Here is the house with spring's lilacs.

First, Bradford lays down a map of LA, layers other papers and materials
on it like a reverse archeology, then he begins the proper archeology

> of stripping, cutting, tearing, exposing, so that the surface of the painting,
> he says, "feels like lacerations, almost like scarring, like bullet wounds."

Yau asks, "What does it mean to be a thing caught in, and carried along,
by time?" The surface of each painting is a skin that suffers the question.

> The skin of rough traces. The skin of marks. One tall letter at a time,
> words appear on the surfaces, like billboard signs annotating the world.

Every image is a piece of information. When he spent a year painting
clouds, Constable looked up at the weather and his own moving mind.

> Each day was an experience of something not sublime, exactly, but entire.
> This is the sky and its clouds. I stand under them. This is its chronicle.

In the still life that will finally contain everything, there will be a coffee
can, a mirror, a seahorse, the *Mona Lisa*. There will be the trumpet,

> the jockstrap, and the roadkill we scavenged for a high school prank,
> my next life gaining in me, like water coursing fiercely up a tree's trunk.

Thoreau said, "The poet writes the history of his own body." The painter
the same. I stand before his painting and understand the solitude that

> is the solitude of the body, as though solitude could be named, as though
> he had left his wallet, glasses, and keys in a shoe by the side of a river.

THE FIELD

Two people are asleep in a field.
The light is not yet up. The air is cold, even though it is summer.
I cannot get closer than where I am. I know only so much
about them. I know they are not dead.
I know they are asleep because one of them has moved, just enough
to show it is a movement you make in sleep, an adjustment
of resting weight. I don't know if it is romantic
that they are in this field. Or if it is drunkenness or despair.
From this distance their clothes are black.
They are two men, or a man and a woman,
or two women. I am not near enough to learn what their bodies are,
or how proximate or distant from each other.
It is the corner of my eye that has seen them,
walking quickly past. It is a corner of my mind that has seen them,
a startled glance, then that glance widening.
They have no belongings, no things that speak of displacement.
The field is askew with untended grass, except where
they have flattened it. Have they been here the full length
of the night, or just the previous hour?
Who are they for whom the grass is a bed? Who are those others,
elsewhere, sleeping in the open back of a truck,
or on the ground behind a guarded fence?
I am walking in the countryside, so maybe they are people of myth.
Or they are people of a labor I know nothing about.
There are birds singing to the dawn. There is the sound
of a big wheel rolling somewhere. There are trees,
as tall as parents, but they have not slept under them.
In the dark, alone, I went out to see the turn toward morning.

Then I saw them. What the imagination would do with two people
sleeping in a field is keep them where they are,
unknowable, untouched. The imagination also wants them
to stir, to wake them back into their stories.
The day will be hot. The smell of yesterday's heat
is still in the air, like the sweat of a body. What would bring me
to a field in the night and have me sleep there?
Whose hand would I be holding, out of desire or fear?
My pants' hems are heavy with dew. I know how far away
I am from everyone. Am I a child again, am I old?
Or am I only who I am now, astounded at the transport of the body
from one end of time to another.

ACKNOWLEDGMENTS

I am grateful to the editors and staff of the following publications, where these poems first appeared: *Adroit Journal* ("Goodwill," "Pleasure"); Academy of American Poets' *Poem-a-Day* ("Moving the Bones"); *Bennington Review* ("To J."); *New England Review* ("Crosshatch 1" and "Crosshatch 2" as "Cross-Hatch"); *New Yorker* ("The Field," "The Lovers"); *New York Times Magazine* ("Of Errands"); *Ocean State Review* ("My Rembrandt"); *Orion* ("The Mussel"); *Poetry* ("The Boy with a Flower Behind His Ear," "The Streets"); *Sepia Journal* ("The Singing"); *Yale Review* ("Abundance").

Much gratitude to Brian Teare and Albion Books for publishing *During the Pandemic* in their chapbook series in 2020. Portions of the sequence have appeared in *Together in a Sudden Strangeness: America's Poets Respond to the Pandemic*, Alfred A. Knopf; *Four Quartets: Poetry in the Pandemic*, Tupelo Press; and *Evergreen: Grim Tales & Verses from the Gloomy Northwest*, Scablands Books.

"Crosshatch 1" and "Crosshatch 2" were written as "Crosshatch" for the Philadelphia Museum of Art, in celebration of its exhibition *Jasper Johns: Mind/ Mirror.* "The Mussel" was written for *Cascadia Field Guide: Art, Ecology, Poetry*, Mountaineers Books. "The Field" was featured on *The Slowdown*.

Thank you to Pacific Lutheran University and MacDowell. And my deep thanks to those who generously gave their time and attention to these poems and this book: Victoria Chang, Oliver de la Paz, Timothy Liu, Brian Teare, Nicholas Templeton, and Monica Youn.

RICK BAROT was born in the Philippines and grew up in the San Francisco Bay Area. He has published four volumes of poetry: *The Darker Fall*; *Want*; *Chord*, which received the UNT Rilke Prize, the PEN Open Book Award, and the Publishing Triangle's Thom Gunn Award; and *The Galleons*, which was on the longlist for the National Book Award in Poetry. His work has appeared in numerous publications, including the *Adroit Journal*, *New England Review*, the *New Yorker*, *Orion*, and *Poetry*. He has received fellowships from the National Endowment for the Arts, The John Simon Guggenheim Memorial Foundation, and Stanford University. He lives in Tacoma, Washington, and directs the Rainier Writing Workshop, the low-residency MFA program in creative writing at Pacific Lutheran University.

milkweed
EDITIONS

Founded as a nonprofit organization in 1980, Milkweed
Editions is an independent publisher. Our mission is to identify,
nurture, and publish transformative literature,
and build an engaged community around it.

Milkweed Editions is based in Bdé Óta Othúŋwe (Minneapolis)
within Mní Sota Makhóčhe, the traditional homeland of
the Dakhóta people. Residing here since time immemorial,
Dakhóta people still call Mní Sota Makhóčhe home, with four
federally recognized Dakhóta nations and many more Dakhóta
people residing in what is now the state of Minnesota. Due to
continued legacies of colonization, genocide, and forced removal,
generations of Dakhóta people remain disenfranchised from
their traditional homeland. Presently, Mní Sota Makhóčhe has
become a refuge and home for many Indigenous nations and
peoples, including seven federally recognized Ojibwe nations.
We humbly encourage our readers to reflect upon the historical
legacies held in the lands they occupy.

milkweed.org